Sport Illustrated

# THE TECHNOLOGY OF

# FOOTBALL

by Shane Frederick

## HIGH-TECH SPORTS

CAPSTONE PRESS
a capstone imprint

Sports Illustrated Kids High-Tech Sports are published by Capstone Press,
1710 Roe Crest Drive, North Mankato, Minnesota 56003
www.capstonepub.com

**Library of Congress Cataloging-in-Publication Data**
Frederick, Shane.
  The technology of football / by Shane Frederick.
    p. cm.—(Sports illustrated kids. High-tech sports)
  Includes bibliographical references and index.
  ISBN 978-1-4296-9953-2 (library binding)
  ISBN 978-1-62065-910-6 (paperback)
1.  Football—Juvenile literature.  I. Title.
GV950.7.F738 2013
796.332—dc23                                    2012033612

**Editorial Credits**
Anthony Wacholtz, editor; Veronica Scott, designer; Eric Gohl, media researcher;
Eric Manske production specialist

**Photo Credits**
AP Images: Amy E. Powers, 13 (top), Darron Cummings, 43, Gene J. Puskar, 27,
Jeff Roberson, 34, Jim Bryant, 30, Mark Humphrey, 42, Michael Thomas, 17, Norwich
Bulletin/John Shishmanian, 25, Robert E. Klein, 22, Seth Wenig, 11; BigStockPhoto.com:
RTimages, cover (background), 1; Corbis: BPI/Joe Toth, 39, Danny Lehman, 12; Courtesy
of Sportvision: 38, 40; Dreamstime: Vishwa Kiran, 33; Getty Images: Michael Zagaris, 32;
Library of Congress: 5 (top); Newscom: Hulteng KRT, 7 (bottom), Image of Sport, 23,
44–45, MCT/Cornett, 15 (bottom), MCT/Jose Carlos Fajardo, 35, Reuters/Brian Snyder,
7 (top), Reuters/Mary Ann Chastain, 9, Reuters/Ray Stubblebine, 19, Reuters/Shaun Best,
15 (top), Staff KRT, 24; *Sports Illustrated*: Al Tielemans, 10 (bottom), 20, 29, Bill Frakes,
36, Bob Rosato, 16, 37, Damian Strohmeyer, 26, Heinz Kluetmeier, 10 (top), John Biever,
cover, 5 (bottom), 31, John W. McDonough, 4, 41, Peter Read Miller, 18, 21, Robert Beck,
13 (bottom), Simon Bruty, 6, 8, 28; Wikipedia: eschipul, 14
Design Elements: Shutterstock

Printed in the United States of America in Stevens Point, Wisconsin.
092012    006937WZS13

# TABLE OF CONTENTS

# FOOTBALL: THE BIG GAME

New York Giants receiver Mario Manningham caught the ball with the tips of his gloves. His toes barely touched down inbounds as New England Patriots safety Patrick Chung flattened him to the turf. Replays of the catch were shown from various angles. The game's referee reviewed the play and determined the call on the field would stand—Manningham's catch was good. It was the biggest play of Super Bowl XLVI. It led to the game-winning touchdown for the Giants. Without modern technology, who knows what would have happened? Would the referee have called the play differently?

Mario Manningham pulls in a catch to keep the game-winning drive alive during the fourth quarter of Super Bowl XLVI.

The origins of American football go back about 150 years. Much has changed since the first official college game was played in 1869. The rules have evolved, and the players have grown bigger and stronger. Tens of thousands of fans fill stadiums every weekend, with millions more watching on TV.

# CHANGING TIMES

While the sport has grown in popularity, it has also evolved with the times. Technology and engineering have altered the way players train for the game, where they play, and the way coaches strategize. It's also made a difference in the way fans watch.

While certain things about today's game are exactly the same as they were in the 1800s, many aspects are unrecognizable from the early days. High-tech uniforms, instant replay, and wireless communication are only a few examples of how the game has evolved.

Let's see how technology has made football what it is today.

# STYLE AND SUBSTANCE

## CHAPTER 1

## HELMETS

Helmets are a major part of the game of football. Headgear helps identify each team—the Cowboys have a star, the Rams have horns, and the Chargers have a lightning bolt. But there is a more important reason that players wear helmets. The helmets keep players safe in a hard-hitting and sometimes violent game.

During the early days, football players didn't wear anything on their heads. It didn't take long for some players to start protecting their heads. The first helmets, made in the late 1800s, were soft leather coverings. Hardened leather was used in the 1930s. In the 1940s the NFL finally made wearing helmets a rule. Today players wear helmets made of hard, shatterproof plastic. The helmets are built to take a blow. Helmets include padding that absorbs energy during a hit or tackle in hopes of reducing serious head injuries.

Equipment companies are always working to make helmets safer. The NFL hopes to have players wearing "smart helmets" with sensors that measure how hard a player has been hit. The sensors would immediately send information to doctors and trainers on the sidelines. They would use that data to see if a player suffered a head injury on the play. The NFL is working with the U.S. Army on the project. The army has used the technology to detect possible brain injuries suffered during combat.

The Xenith X2 helmet helps players avoid head injury. Shock absorbers cushion a player's head during a hard hit.

# EVOLUTION OF THE FOOTBALL HELMET

*As football has become more sophisticated, the function and structure of helmets have changed. The helmet's evolution since the earliest days of the National Football League:*

### 1920s
Head completely covered for first time; improved padding at crown, reinforced leather bands across top

### 1940s
Modified leather helmets gradually replaced by plastic ones, which become conventional by late 1940s

### 1930s
Some helmets are modified to a boxer's training headgear; colors are introduced

### 1950s
Shatter-prone lucite face mask gives way to masks with bars

### 1960s
Inside of helmet re-engineered to protect head better

### 1970s
Plastic shell reinforced for protection in an increasingly physical game; face masks continue evolving

### Today
Hard plastic shell, inflatable liner to protect against head injury; face shield varies by position

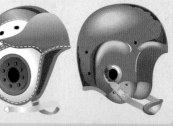

SOURCE: Pro Football Hall of Fame, N.Y. Giants, Riddell

Shoulder pads are made of a hard plastic shell over foam padding. They're designed to absorb the shock of hitting another player. When a player gets tackled to the turf, the energy of the hit is distributed throughout his pads. That way, the impact is less painful and injuries can be avoided.

Over time equipment designers have improved the protective padding that players wear on their shoulders, hips, thighs, and knees. Today's pads are stronger and lighter than ever. Unlike decades ago, shoulder pads are designed specifically for certain positions. Quarterbacks' pads often include an attached **flak jacket**. The flak jacket protects a quarterback's ribs and back from dangerous hits. The jacket still allows him enough mobility to run and throw the ball well.

Carolina Panthers
quarterback
Cam Newton

flak jacket—special padding designed to protect the chest and back

# CATCHING THE BALL

In the late 1970s some players slathered a sticky goo called Stickum on their hands and jerseys in order to get a better grip on the ball. But in 1981 the NFL banned the product and other gluelike substances during games. The league stated it was unfair to use such substances.

Lester Hayes spreads Stickum on his hands during Super Bowl XV.

Players didn't give up looking for an advantage, though. San Francisco 49ers receiver Jerry Rice tried to use gloves

worn by scuba divers, but they were too thick and bulky. Today almost all receivers and many other players wear special gloves designed specifically for football. They are lightweight, and the palms and fingers are made of a tacky, flexible, water-resistant material that helps players hold on to the ball. The high-tech gloves probably prevented wide receiver Santonio Holmes from dropping the ball during a tiptoe catch during Super Bowl XLIII. His spectacular catch made the Pittsburgh Steelers champions of the 2008 season.

# HIGH-TECH JERSEYS

Before the 2012 season, the NFL unveiled new jerseys designed to be lighter, drier, and cooler. They were made of material that wicks away sweat from the inside and repels rain on the outside. Also, the jerseys were designed to wrap tight around the pads, making them tough for opponents to grab.

# AT THE STADIUM

## CHAPTER 2

## ON THE FIELD

Football is no longer strictly an outdoor game like it was in its early days. The sport began moving indoors in the late 1960s with the construction of the Houston Astrodome. The arena was the home of the Houston Oilers and known at the time as the Eighth Wonder of the World.

During its first year, the Astrodome had natural grass. But the grass didn't grow very well indoors and most of it died. That led to the creation of Astroturf.

About the only thing natural grass and the original Astroturf had in common was their green color. The Astroturf's carpetlike surface was rough and hard. The rough surface led to many injuries, from rug-burned skin to torn knee ligaments. But it was also popular, and several stadiums—both indoor and outdoor—used it. Teams took advantage of the synthetic turf's fast-playing surface by drafting speedier receivers and other skill players.

The Astrodome

Over time technology has improved artificial turf. Today 14 NFL teams play on Field Turf or something similar. The new-age surface is designed to look and feel like natural grass and has real ground underneath.

## WHAT IS FIELD TURF?

- Woven, fabric backing
- Infill of **silica** sand and **cryogenic** rubber made from recycled tires
- Grasslike fibers stitched into the backing

## COLORFUL TURF

Who says artificial turf has to be green? While most synthetic fields are made to look like natural grass, Boise State University opted to go with its school colors. The university has had blue turf at Bronco Stadium for more than 25 years.

**silica**—a chemical found in sand
**cryogenic**—describes something produced using very low temperatures

# MORE THAN A DOME

Eighteen NFL teams play on grass today. Thanks to technology and engineering, that group includes two teams that play indoors.

Reliant Stadium replaced the Astrodome in 2002. The home of the Houston Texans was the first of four NFL stadiums to have retractable roofs. The roofs cover the stadium but can be opened and closed mechanically.

The Texans keep the roof open to allow the natural-grass field to grow thick and strong. When the weather is nice, it stays open for games too. But the roof also closes in bad weather or on hot, humid Houston days. On those days the stadium is air conditioned for the fans' comfort.

A crew prepared the field at the University of Phoenix Stadium before it was rolled inside for Super Bowl XLII in 2008.

The Arizona Cardinals' University of Phoenix Stadium has a retractable roof. But it also has something no other NFL stadium has—a retractable field! Grass grows on a 2-acre (0.8-hectare) tray that sits outside of the stadium in Glendale, Arizona. Before game day, the tray and field rolls into the building, using 546 wheels that move on 16 tracks. It goes 0.13 miles (0.21 kilometers) per hour and takes 75 minutes to move into place.

## The unfrozen tundra

*How technology helps keep Lambeau Field, home of the Green Bay Packers, in championship shape:*

**How system works**

**1** Soil warming system, installed in 1997, combines **natural grass, synthetic turf**; synthetic portion uses strands that extend below surface with 1 inch (2.54 cm) exposed

**2** Eight-inch (20.3 cm) **transition zone** helps to stabilize natural grass roots

**3** Twelve inches (30.5 cm) of **sand** is fitted below transition zone

**4** **Clay base** sits below sand; radiant heating pipe is fed by a hot-water boiler, heating grass roots to 70°F (21°C) during the winter

Source: Tweet/Garrot, Gas Utility Report, Post-Crescent (Appleton, Wis.), Green Bay Packers Graphic: Richard Cornett, Newsday

Synthetic strands     Natural grass

8 in. (20.3 cm)

12 in. (30.5 cm)

Heating pipe          © 2008 MCT

Even open-air stadiums use technology to keep the grass growing. At Lambeau Field in Green Bay, Wisconsin, more than 30 miles (48 km) of heating pipe are buried in the soil. The piping keeps the grass growing and the turf from freezing late in the season.

# THE FAN EXPERIENCE

There was a time when a ticket for an NFL game gave a person no more than a seat in the stadium and the hope to see his or her favorite team win. Today there is so much more for people to see and do. Teams continue to add things to their stadiums to make game day even better for the fans.

Cowboys Stadium in Arlington, Texas, has more than 100,000 seats and boasts the world's largest retractable roof. It's also home to the NFL's two largest TV screens. Hanging 90 feet (27 meters) above the field, the high-definition Jumbotrons stretch 2,100 inches (5,330 cm)—almost 60 yards (55 m)!

Cowboys Stadium

Each end of the 600-ton (544-metric ton) display has a 700-inch (1,780-cm) screen facing the end zones. Most fans can see the action more clearly on the Jumbrotrons than on the field.

Fans who don't want to watch the big screens can use the small screens on their smartphones, tablets, and devices available for rent at the games. Several teams are working to create apps that allow fans in the stadium to call up instant replays on demand. Cowboys Stadium, for instance, has more than 15 camera angles to choose from.

Fans at Cowboys Stadium can watch special broadcasts in 3D using special glasses.

## FACT

The Cowboys' big screens above the field have tempted several punters into trying to kick a ball high enough to hit them. One punter actually succeeded! Tennessee Titans backup A.J. Trapasso hit the bottom of the Jumbotron with a punt during a preseason game. Officials knew what to do, though. The NFL had already changed its rules to make any punt that hit the screen a dead ball, and Trapasso had to punt again.

# THE 12TH MAN

Each football team has 11 players on the field at a time. However, the "12th man" often is praised for helping a team win. The so-called extra player is the home crowd and the noise that the fans make during a game.

In Seattle, Washington, the Seahawks credit their home-field advantage for frequently causing opposing offensive players to jump offsides for false-start penalties. Seahawks fans have been some of the NFL's loudest since they began playing in the Kingdome, the team's home for about 24 years. When the open-air Seahawks Stadium was built in the early 2000s, it was engineered to be the loudest stadium in the NFL.

The stands are close to the field, and a partial roof over the seats reflects the cheering back on the field. Noise has been measured as loud as 135 **decibels**—nearly the same as the sound a jet engine makes at takeoff and more than enough to cause hearing damage.

MetLife Stadium was designed to conserve energy and resources.

# "GREEN" STADIUMS

MetLife Stadium, the shared home field of the New York Giants and New York Jets, opened in 2010. It was engineered as an eco-friendly building with designs to conserve energy and water. It was built with 20,000 tons (18,140 metric tons) of steel recycled from the old Giants Stadium. Following the first season of play, plans were put in place to begin using solar energy to help power the stadium.

decibel—a unit for measuring how loud a sound is

## CHAPTER 3

## PREPARING TO PLAY

Football players do many things to try to gain the edge in competition. They lift weights, run sprints, and eat right to keep their bodies ready for peak performance come game day.

Many NFL players build their acceleration by running with weights attached to a harness. Faster acceleration can help safeties, such as former Jacksonville Jaguar Donovin Darius, gain a few extra steps to intercept a quarterback's pass.

But it's not just about training muscles. Some players even train their eyes to see better! Receivers recently started training with special glasses to help their focus and concentration. The glasses have **LCD** lenses that cloud the wearer's vision with patterns and force the player to concentrate on finding and catching the ball. As Pittsburgh Steelers star defensive back Troy Polamalu said: "You gotta play the game with your eyes."

Troy Polamalu

## FACT

Players, coaches, and scouts want to know everything they can about how the athletes perform. A new gadget sewn into a workout shirt contains a sensor that transmits all sorts of data to a computer. It measures a player's heart rate, breathing rate, acceleration while sprinting, and direction changes.

LCD—a type of TV screen; LCD stands for liquid crystal display

# CAUGHT ON TAPE

It seems you can't go anywhere today without the chance of being videotaped. The football field is no exception. Not only are all of the games televised, but every NFL team shoots video of all of their practices—and from many angles.

A video technician recorded an overhead view of the New England Patriots' training camp.

# HELMET CAM

Some teams have begun using a camera attached to the front or side of a helmet during practice to study how a quarterback reads the defense before he makes a throw. When coaches and players watch the recording, they can see what the quarterback saw on the play. Did he find the safeties lurking in the backfield? Did he notice that the man he threw to was double covered? Did he see the open receiver streaking down the sideline?

St. Louis Rams running back Steven Jackson

Having video of practice allows coaches to study plays and make sure their players are running them correctly. It also allows players to focus on their own skills, body movements, and techniques.

Through video analysis computer software, a quarterback can review his throwing motion and find out how he can add zip to his passes. An offensive lineman can study his footwork to make himself a better blocker. And a punter can make sure he's getting a high enough leg kick to pin the opponents deep in their own territory.

In 2001 Minnesota Vikings offensive lineman Korey Stringer died hours after suffering heat stroke during the team's summer training camp. Stringer's 335-pound (152-kilogram) body rose in temperature from the normal 98.6 degrees Fahrenheit (37 degrees Celsius) to more than 108 F (42 C) and couldn't be cooled down. Before he collapsed, the Vikings' doctors and trainers did not suspect Stringer was in danger. Today there is a way for players to be monitored and better protected from the heat.

## Tracking player temperatures

*Some NFL teams already use a system that features vitamin-sized "radio pills" to monitor players' core body temperatures during practice.*

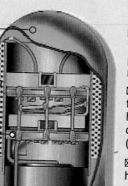

### The pill

Outer silicone coat

Communication coils

Temperature sensing crystal

Battery

### How it works

☒ Player swallows "pill" the night before practice or early the next morning

☒ Pill transmits up to 300 ft. (90 m) to handheld personal digital assistant (shown below)

☒ Pills last 24-36 hours before passing out of the human body

### Personal digital assistant

☒ PDA displays data in real time for each player

☒ System has high temperature alert feature

☒ System monitors up to 99 players at one time

Players can swallow a pill that contains a tiny thermometer and radio transmitter before practice. Throughout the workout, trainers can use a scanner to retrieve the radio signal and find the player's core temperature. If his temperature is rising, the player can rest and cool down.

With the growing concern of head injuries, there are better tests in place to monitor concussions. Concussions are brain injuries usually caused by blows to the head. They can cause serious problems, including dizziness, headaches, blurred vision, and memory loss. Football players can get concussions from being hit in the head by another player, especially by the player's helmet. A concussion can also happen if a player hits his head on the ground.

High school football players take a baseline concussion test.

Players take a computer test called ImPACT before the season begins to get a baseline score of how their brains are functioning. If they suffer a concussion, they retake that test. The scores are then compared to see if and when the player can return to the field.

## CHAPTER 4

## GETTING IT RIGHT

As much as technology has enhanced football, it is still played, coached, and officiated by humans. None of those people are perfect at what they do, no matter how hard they try.

Referees have the job of making sure a lightning-fast, hard-hitting game is played according to the rules. It's not an easy job. That's why the NFL has taken advantage of instant-replay technology to help the refs make the right calls. It helped confirm that Mario Manningham's Super Bowl catch was indeed a legal one.

Sometimes home-field advantage can help a team challenge a play. Some coaches will watch the replay on the stadium's big screen before deciding whether a challenge is worthwhile. But there are times when the replay is put up quickly for the home coach but perhaps not in time for the visiting team.

A head coach throws a red flag onto the field to challenge a play. The coach must challenge the call before the next play starts.

The referee can review all scoring plays and turnovers. For all other close plays, such as receptions and out-of-bounds spots, the call must be challenged by one of the head coaches. Each coach gets two challenges per game. A third challenge is awarded if the coach is correct on his first two. If the coach is wrong, his team loses one of its valuable timeouts. If a team is out of timeouts, it cannot challenge a play. However, during the last two minutes of each half and overtime, a replay official decides whether to look at a play. Coaches' challenges aren't allowed during that time.

To review the play, the ref goes into a small booth on the sideline and watches the play on a TV monitor. He can watch the play from many camera angles. But he only has a certain amount of time to review the play before he has to announce if the original call stands or if it's reversed.

# CALLING THE PLAYS

Communication is important in all sports, and in football there are several coaches and players scattered throughout the stadium to keep on top of things. The head coach is on the sideline. His offensive and defensive coordinators may be in a booth high above the field. The quarterback is on the field. How do they talk to each other? Through wireless technology.

New York Jets head coach Rex Ryan (center) uses a wireless microphone to communicate with the quarterback and other team coaches.

Coaches wear headsets with microphones during games. They talk to one another through the devices. They also send plays to the quarterback, who hears the call through a speaker in his helmet. The signal to the quarterback is synced with the play clock and cuts out when 15 seconds remain before the ball must be snapped. As radio technology has improved, communication has become clearer between coaches and players, even in loud stadiums.

Linebacker Brian Urlacher (54) relays the upcoming play to the rest of the team.

For many years the quarterback was the only player on the field to have a radio in his helmet. Starting in 2008 rules made it fair for both sides, giving one defensive player a radio helmet. Players no longer had to run in plays from the sideline or use hand signals or signs.

Some wonder if there will be a day when all players have a receiver in their helmets. Would that mean the end of the huddle?

# BREAKING DOWN FILM

Practice is important for teams and players to prepare for the upcoming game. But running plays and working on fundamentals aren't enough to win a game. Coaches and players study video of games and practices to analyze exactly what is going on during a play or a drill.

Some teams have a film review room for each player position.

Two cameras videotape each NFL game—one with a sideline view and another with an end zone angle. The film is distributed to all of the teams. The tape is often called the "All 22" because every player can be seen on the screen.

Coaches and players watch the films over and over again in meeting rooms, as well as on laptop computers and DVD players. They study themselves and their upcoming opponents to find out what goes right and what goes wrong on a given play.

# GOING TOO FAR

There are rules and limitations when it comes to filming. In 2007 the New England Patriots were caught videotaping another team's defensive signals during a game. Some called it spying. Others called it cheating. Either way, the NFL didn't approve. The league punished the team and coach Bill Belichick by fining them hundreds of thousands of dollars and by taking away a first-round draft pick.

Bill Belichick (center) and the New England Patriots

# SIDELINE TECHNOLOGY

There are rules outlining
when players are allowed
to use personal electronic
devices such as iPads.

Although technology drives football into the future, the sport sometimes seems stuck in the past on the sidelines. Quarterbacks and other players study large black-and-white photographs taken just before and just after each snap. Coaches and coordinators often have their plays listed on large laminated cards.

So why aren't teams taking advantage of modern technology on the sidelines? Computers, personal digital assistants (PDAs), and other electronic devices like iPads can only be used in certain areas. They are not allowed on the sidelines, the booths, or the locker rooms before and during a game. The NFL doesn't want teams to have an unfair advantage during games. All teams would have to have access to the exact same technology.

Some people hope those rules will change. Perhaps we'll see a time when the quarterback examines pictures or even video of play on a tablet, rather than waiting for a collection of photos to print out. Maybe a coach can keep his playbook in and even make calls from a handheld device.

## DIGITAL PLAYBOOK

While computer tablets aren't yet allowed on sidelines, teams are finding other ways to use them. Instead of giving players thick binders full of pages of plays to study, some coaches are putting their playbooks on team-owned iPads. Players can also use an app to study film on the tablet.

# BETTER AT HOME?

## CHAPTER 5

## THE BROADCAST REVOLUTION

It didn't take long for someone to realize that not everyone interested in football had a ticket to a game. By the 1920s and 1930s, football could be heard on the radio throughout the country. Radio is still a popular way for fans to follow football today. You can listen to a game in the car or while spending time outdoors on a nice day. But watching televised football might be the most popular activity in America. Three recent Super Bowls—XLVI, XLV and XLIV—rank as the top three most-watched TV programs of all time, with more than 110 million people watching in 2011 and 2012.

Today every NFL game is televised throughout the season. Devoted football fans can pay to have access to every game through satellite TV or cable. If viewers are only interested in seeing touchdowns, the NFL has a RedZone channel that switches from game to game depending on when a team gets into scoring range.

John Madden, a retired NFL coach and former commentator, likes to watch games in style. His main TV is 16 feet (4.9 m) long and 9 feet (2.7 m) high. The mammoth TV is surrounded by eight 63-inch (160-cm) screens.

## FACT

On October 22, 1939, NBC became the first network to televise an NFL game. It was a matchup between the Philadelphia Eagles and the Brooklyn Dodgers at Ebbets Field in Brooklyn, New York. The Dodgers won the game 23-14.

# TECHNOLOGY JUST FOR YOU

The first televised football games used only two cameras to show the action to fans at home. More than 70 years later, networks used 20 times as many cameras to capture the action. During its broadcast of Super Bowl XLVI between the New York Giants and the New England Patriots, NBC used 57 cameras! Forty of those were used for game coverage, while the other 17 were used in pregame and postgame shows.

One camera moves along a wire above the field to capture an overhead shot of the game.

The cameras are located throughout the stadium. There's even one that that zips back and forth along a high wire over the players' heads. The cameras don't miss much. When there's a key interception, viewers are able to see a variety of angles. They might see a wide shot on the field, a close-up of the battle between a defensive back and a wide receiver, and views of what the quarterback saw (or didn't see) on the play. They might even see the reaction of both head coaches on the sidelines.

Aerial camera

The pictures all flow together nicely during a broadcast, but it's not easy. A director and a production crew piece the videos together from a trailer parked outside the stadium. They have to monitor all of the camerawork, watching as many as 100 TV screens.

# TV TOOLS

The first instant replay shown during a football broadcast came during the 1963 Army-Navy game. Since then many broadcast gadgets have been added to give TV viewers a better understanding of the game.

## Here are a few:

**FREEZE FRAME:** Stops the action at a certain point in a play, perhaps to see a key block that opened a hole for a running back. Digital, high-definition close-ups can show if a receiver kept his feet inbounds during a sideline catch.

**GRAPHICS:** Give details about the game, including an on-screen scoreboard, game clock and play clock, and statistical information.

BCS on FOX | FLA 21 | OSU 14 | 6:11 2ND | 3RD & 15 | Tostitos BCS CHAMPIONSHIP

3RD & 15

7 PLAYS, 32 YDS, 2:53

**TELESTRATOR:** Allows the TV analyst to draw a play on the screen or circle players viewers should watch during the replay.

**SUPER SLOW-MO:** Gives viewers a chance to watch a play unfold in slow motion so they can pick out details and better understand what happened.

**MICROPHONES:** Capture some of the discussions that take place during a game. Sideline microphones pick up a quarterback's signals and snap counts. Some players even agree to wear small microphones inside their pads.

The large half bubble around a microphone acts like a funnel, catching sounds from on the field.

# THE THIN YELLOW LINE

One of the most advanced pieces of technology in football was created specifically for fans watching from home. The yellow first-down line helps viewers know what yard line a team must get to for a first down.

An offensive team gets four plays called downs to move the ball at least 10 yards. If a team does that, it gets a first down and four more downs to go another 10 yards.

While the idea of putting a computer-generated line on a TV screen seems simple, it's not. It takes eight computers and four people to make it work properly.

Since each stadium is different, the computers need to know where all the cameras are and how they relate to every line on the field. They need to know how the cameras zoom in and out and how they move. They also need to know the difference between the grass and a player, so the line stays behind the people on the field during the broadcast.

## MOVING THE CHAINS

Because referees don't use TV screens except for replays, first downs are measured on the field with a 10-yard long metal chain connected to two poles. The people holding the poles during the game are often called the chain gang.

# CHANGING HOW WE WATCH

Ready to kick back on the couch and watch your favorite football team play a game? It's no longer enough to have the remote control in one hand and a bowl of popcorn in the other. Today you might watch a game with a laptop computer open on the coffee table and a tablet, such as an iPad, or a smartphone ready for action. That's because the game isn't just happening on the big screen across the room. Today's football fan is more connected than ever.

Tennessee Titans linebacker Keith Bullock on his laptop after a practice

Pro football games have become a center for many social media outlets, from Facebook to Twitter.

Fans have instant access to statistics and other information. They can follow their fantasy football teams in real time, tracking touchdowns and yardage just moments after they happen. They can go on the Web and read a live analysis of games by newspaper reporters, columnists, and other experts. Fans can also log on to Twitter and interact with other fans who are watching the same game.

## FACT

During the 2012 Pro Bowl, the NFL set up Twitter stations on the sidelines so players could type in their thoughts about the game between plays.

# THE FUTURE OF FOOTBALL

Just like the players of 1869 could not have pictured what football would look like in the 2000s, it's hard to predict what the NFL will look like in 2150. Will it be at all similar to today's version of the game? One thing we do know: Technology is always moving forward and advances often find their way to sports. Studies are continually being done to improve training, replay, and fan enjoyment.

Researchers are hoping to one day put a **GPS** unit in the football to get an exact spot of the ball once the play ends. That could help determine whether a touchdown was scored amid a big pile on the goal line or whether a first down was gained on a key play late in the game. Researchers are also looking into sensors in gloves that might help officials tell the difference between a catch, an incomplete pass, and a fumble. Others are hoping to use video-game technology to digitally animate game film in order to get different views of why plays worked and why they didn't. They're not there yet, but it's exciting to think about what might be ahead for pro football.

**GPS**—satellite-based technology that pinpoints specific locations; GPS stands for global positioning system

# GLOSSARY

**app**—a computer program for a tablet or smartphone; app is short for application

**concussion**—an injury to the brain caused by a blow to or a jarring of the head

**conserve**—to use something carefully to prevent loss or waste

**coordinator**—in football, the top assistant offensive or defensive coach

**cryogenic**—describes something produced using very low temperatures

**decibel**—a unit for measuring how loud a sound is

**engineering**—the work of designing structures, products, and systems

**flak jacket**—special padding designed to protect the chest and back

**GPS**—satellite-based technology that pinpoints specific locations; GPS stands for global positioning system

**huddle**—a gathering of football players on a team before a play

**LCD**—a type of TV screen; LCD stands for liquid crystal display

**mobility**—the ability to move quickly and easily

**retractable**—able to be pulled back or opened

**sensor**—a device that detects change, such as heat, light, sound, or motion

**silica**—a chemical found in sand

**synthetic**—not natural

**tacky**—slightly sticky

**wick**—to cause moisture to be pulled away from a surface

# READ MORE

**Levine, Shar, and Leslie Johnstone.** *Sports Science.* New York: Sterling Pub., 2006.

**Slade, Suzanne.** *Basketball: How It Works.* Mankato, Minn.: Capstone Press, 2010.

**Solway, Andrew.** *Sports Science.* Chicago: Heinemann Library, 2009.

**Tomecek, Stephen.** *Sports.* New York: Chelsea House, 2010.

# INTERNET SITES

FactHound offers a safe, fun way to find Internet sites related to this book. All of the sites on FactHound have been researched by our staff.

Here's all you do:

Visit *www.facthound.com*

Type in this code: 9781429699532

Super-cool stuff!

Check out projects, games and lots more at
**www.capstonekids.com**

# INDEX